"Freelance Pro Secrets: Guide to a Successful Solo Career"

Aura Marx

INTRODUCTION

Welcome to the thrilling world of freelancing, a realm where your career is driven by your passions, skills, and the sheer joy of crafting your destiny. The landscape of work has transformed dramatically over the years, and at the heart of this evolution is freelancing. Once seen as the road less traveled, it has burgeoned into a vibrant, bustling highway of opportunities, playing a pivotal role in the global economy. This isn't just about picking up odd jobs anymore; it's about building a career on your terms, with the freedom to choose who you work with, what projects you dive into, and where you set up your office—even if it's on a beach in Bali!

Gone are the days when '9 to 5' was the only melody to our work lives. The freelance industry has blossomed, fueled by technology that connects us across continents and a cultural shift towards valuing flexibility and autonomy. This revolution isn't just a tiny ripple; it's a tidal wave reshaping industries and opening doors to new ways of working. Freelancers are no longer the outliers; they are integral players in the economy, bringing their unique skills to a global marketplace thirsty for talent.

Now, you might wonder, "Why choose freelancing?" Imagine having the power to design your day, select projects that ignite your passion, and work with clients from around the globe—all while wearing your favorite pajamas. Sounds dreamy, right? But it's not just about comfort; it's about crafting a career that aligns with your life goals and values. Freelancing offers unparalleled flexibility, allowing you to balance work with personal pursuits, whether that's traveling the world or spending more time with your family.

But there's more to it than just convenience. Freelancing is a journey of self-discovery and growth. It pushes you to hone your skills, adapt to new challenges, and continuously evolve. You're not just building a portfolio; you're sculpting a brand that's uniquely you. This path empowers you to take charge of your career, explore diverse projects, and connect with like-minded individuals who share your passion for creativity and innovation.

So, as we embark on this journey through "Freelance Pro Secrets," keep your mind open to the endless possibilities that freelancing offers. Whether you're a seasoned freelancer or just dipping your toes into these waters, this book is your compass, guiding you towards a successful and fulfilling solo career.

Chapter 1

Setting the Foundation

Embarking on a freelance career is akin to setting off on an epic adventure—one where you're both the hero and the navigator. But before you chart your course through this exhilarating world, let's lay down the groundwork. Understanding the essence of freelancing and nurturing the right mindset are your initial steps towards a rewarding solo career.

Understanding Freelancing: The Art of Being Your Own Boss

Freelancing is more than a career choice; it's a lifestyle. It's about embracing the freedom to choose your projects, your clients, and your schedule. But with great freedom comes great responsibility. As a freelancer, you're the CEO, the marketing department, the finance manager, and the workforce, all rolled into one. You're in charge of finding work, completing projects, billing clients, and, yes, making sure you get paid on time. It's about self-management and discipline, ensuring that you can sustain your business and your livelihood.

But what truly sets freelancing apart is the sheer diversity of opportunities it presents. Whether you're a writer, a designer, a developer, or a consultant, freelancing allows you to carve out a niche based on your skills and passions. It's about finding your unique place in the vast digital marketplace, where your talents meet the needs of clients from around the globe.

Mindset for Success:
Cultivating Your Inner Freelancer

The cornerstone of a flourishing freelance career is the right mindset. It's about more than just skill; it's about how you approach your work and your life. Here are some key mindset shifts to consider:

Embrace Flexibility: In freelancing, adaptability is your best friend. Projects, clients, and income can fluctuate, and being flexible allows you to navigate these changes with grace. It's about being open to new opportunities and willing to pivot when necessary.

Cultivate Discipline: Without the structure of a traditional job, managing your time effectively becomes crucial. It's about setting your own deadlines, staying focused, and keeping procrastination at bay. Remember, discipline is what turns potential into success.

Foster Resilience: Not every project will go smoothly, and not every pitch will land you a gig. Resilience is about bouncing back from setbacks, learning from each experience, and moving forward with renewed determination.

Commit to Continuous Learning: The freelance world is ever-evolving, and staying ahead means being a lifelong learner. Whether it's honing your existing skills or acquiring new ones, continuous learning is the fuel that drives your freelance career forward.

Value Your Worth: One of the most significant shifts is recognizing the value you bring to the table. It's about setting fair rates for your work and advocating for yourself in negotiations. Remember, you're offering valuable skills and deserve to be compensated accordingly.

Building a Solid Foundation

As you step into the freelance arena, remember that you're building more than a business; you're crafting a career that reflects your values, your passions, and your lifestyle. Here are a few foundational steps to start on the right foot:

Define Your Services: Clearly articulate what you offer. Whether it's writing compelling content, designing stunning graphics, or developing innovative software, know your strengths and how they translate into services for your clients.

Identify Your Ideal Clients: Not every client is a good fit. Define who your ideal clients are—what industries they're in, what problems they're facing, and how your skills can solve those problems. This clarity will help you target your marketing efforts effectively.

Set Up Your Workspace: Whether it's a home office, a co-working space, or your kitchen table, create a workspace that inspires productivity and creativity. Having a dedicated work area can help you establish a routine and keep your work life separate from your personal life.

Get Your Finances in Order: Freelancing also means managing your finances. Set up a system for tracking your income and expenses, invoicing clients, and saving for taxes. Consider consulting with a financial advisor to ensure you're on the right track.

As you embark on this journey, remember that freelancing is a marathon, not a sprint. It's about building a career that's not only successful but also fulfilling and aligned with your life goals. So take a deep breath, set your sights on the horizon, and take that first step with confidence. Your freelance adventure awaits!

Mindset for Success:

Cultivating the right attitude and mindset essential for thriving in the freelance world.

As you embark on your freelance journey, remember that your most powerful tool isn't the latest software or even your skill set; it's your mindset. The way you view challenges, your work, and even yourself can profoundly influence your path in the freelance world. Let's dive into the core attitudes and mindsets that pave the way for a successful and fulfilling freelance career.

Embracing the Growth Mindset

In the realm of freelancing, the only constant is change. Projects come and go, technologies evolve, and client needs shift. Thriving in such a dynamic environment requires a growth mindset. This means seeing every challenge as an opportunity to learn and grow, rather than a roadblock. It's about asking, "What can I learn from this?" instead of lamenting, "Why is this happening to me?" Cultivating this mindset empowers you to navigate the ups and downs of freelancing with resilience and grace.

Adaptability: Your Secret Weapon

Freelancing will test your ability to adapt like nothing else. You might be juggling projects with varying deadlines, working with clients from different cultures, or needing to learn new skills on the fly. Adaptability is about staying flexible and open to new ways of working. It's about crafting creative solutions when the usual approaches don't cut it. By staying adaptable, you ensure that you can ride the waves of change rather than being swept away by them.

Self-Discipline: The Freelancer's Foundation

Without the external structure of a traditional office environment, self-discipline becomes the backbone of your freelance career. It's about setting your own deadlines, managing your time effectively, and holding yourself accountable. But self-discipline isn't just about work; it's also about knowing when to take a break, to prevent burnout. It's the delicate balance between pushing yourself to achieve and listening to your needs.

Resilience: Bouncing Back Stronger

The freelance journey is not without its bumps. There will be times when proposals are rejected, feedback is tough, or projects fall through. Resilience is the ability to bounce back from these setbacks, not allowing them to define you or derail your journey. It's about learning from each experience and using it to build a stronger, more robust freelance practice. Remember, every "no" brings you closer to the next "yes."

The Power of a Positive Attitude

Maintaining a positive attitude isn't about ignoring the challenges of freelancing; it's about choosing to focus on the opportunities and solutions. It's about celebrating your wins, no matter how small, and maintaining a sense of gratitude for the journey you're on. A positive attitude attracts positive outcomes and can make you a magnet for clients and collaborators who value your energy and outlook.

Continuous Learning: Staying Ahead of the Curve

The freelance world moves fast, and staying relevant means committing to continuous learning. Whether it's keeping up with industry trends, mastering new tools, or developing soft skills like communication and negotiation, the most successful freelancers are perpetual students. View each project as a learning opportunity and invest in your professional development. Your future self will thank you.

Networking: Building Relationships, Not Just Contacts

In freelancing, your network is your net worth. But effective networking isn't just about collecting business cards; it's about building genuine relationships. It's about connecting with others on a human level, offering value, and supporting each other's growth. Approach networking with a mindset of abundance, believing there's enough work for everyone, and focus on how you can help others succeed.

Self-Care: The Freelancer's Best Investment

Finally, it's essential to recognize that taking care of yourself is not a luxury; it's a necessity. Managing your energy, prioritizing your health, and setting boundaries are crucial for sustaining a long and successful freelance career. Remember, you are your business's most valuable asset. When you thrive, your business thrives.

Crafting Your Mindset Masterpiece

As you move forward, think of cultivating your mindset as an ongoing process, a masterpiece you're continuously painting. With each stroke of resilience, each shade of positivity, and each hue of discipline, you're creating a mindset that not only supports your freelance career but also enriches your life. Remember, the right mindset is the foundation upon which all your freelance successes are built. So nurture it, cherish it, and watch as it transforms your freelance journey into an adventure of growth, fulfillment, and endless possibilities

Chapter 2

Building Your Brand

In the vast ocean of the freelance world, your personal brand is the lighthouse that guides clients to your shore. It's more than just a logo or a catchy tagline; it's the essence of who you are, what you stand for, and the unique value you bring to the table. Building a strong personal brand is about crafting a narrative that resonates with your ideal clients, setting you apart in a crowded marketplace. Let's embark on this journey to build a brand that's authentically you and irresistibly attractive to those you aim to serve.

The Heart of Your Brand: Authenticity

The foundation of any strong brand is authenticity. In a world where everyone is trying to stand out, your true power lies in being yourself. Your personal brand should be a reflection of your values, your passions, and your unique approach to your work. It's about sharing your story in a way that connects with others on a personal level. When you're authentic, you attract clients who appreciate not just your work, but who you are as a person, making for more enjoyable and fulfilling collaborations.

Crafting Your Unique Value Proposition (UVP)

At the core of your personal brand is your Unique Value Proposition—the special sauce that makes you, well, you. It's the answer to the question, "Why should a client choose me over someone else?" Your UVP could be your distinctive style, your approach to solving problems, or the unique blend of skills you bring to the table. Identifying and articulating your UVP is crucial; it's what you'll communicate through your marketing materials, your portfolio, and even the way you talk about your work.

Visual Identity: The Face of Your Brand

Humans are visual creatures, and the visual elements of your brand play a key role in making a lasting impression. This includes your logo, color scheme, typography, and overall aesthetic. These elements should be consistent across all your platforms, from your website to your social media profiles to your business cards. A cohesive visual identity not only makes you look professional but also makes you instantly recognizable, reinforcing your brand in the minds of potential clients.

Online Presence: Your Digital Storefront

In today's digital age, your online presence is often the first point of contact between you and your potential clients. A professional website acts as your digital storefront, showcasing your portfolio, your services, and your brand personality. It's your opportunity to make a strong first impression, tell your story, and convince clients that you're the right person for the job. Alongside your website, your social media channels offer a platform to share your insights, highlight your projects, and engage with your community, further solidifying your brand.

Content Creation: Sharing Your Voice

Content is king, and creating valuable, engaging content is a powerful way to build your brand. Whether it's blog posts, videos, podcasts, or social media updates, sharing your knowledge and insights positions you as an authority in your field. It's about providing value to your audience, helping them solve problems, and enriching their lives. When you consistently create content that resonates with your audience, you not only enhance your brand but also build trust with potential clients.

Networking and Collaboration: Expanding Your Brand's Reach

Building a personal brand isn't a solo journey. Networking and collaborating with others in your industry can amplify your brand's reach. Attend industry events, join online communities, and collaborate on projects with peers. Each interaction is an opportunity to showcase your brand and make meaningful connections. Remember, your network is an extension of your brand, so nurture these relationships with the same care and authenticity you put into your work.

Feedback and Adaptation: Evolving Your Brand

Your personal brand is not set in stone; it's a living, breathing entity that evolves with you. Regularly seek feedback from clients, peers, and mentors, and be open to adapting your brand as you grow. Perhaps your interests shift, you develop new skills, or you discover new insights about your target audience. Embracing these changes and updating your brand accordingly ensures that it always represents the best and most current version of you.

Building a Brand That Resonates

As you build your personal brand, remember that it's about more than just attracting clients; it's about connecting with people on a deeper level. It's the story you tell, the value you offer, and the relationships you build. With each step you take in crafting your brand, you're not just enhancing your business; you're enriching the community you serve. So infuse your brand with your personality, your passion, and your purpose, and watch as it opens doors to opportunities you never imagined.

Personal Branding 101: The Art of Standing Out

In the bustling freelance marketplace, where talent abounds and competition is fierce, how do you shine brightly enough to catch the eye of your ideal clients? The answer lies in the mastery of personal branding. It's not just about being seen; it's about being remembered, chosen, and cherished. Let's unravel the mysteries of personal branding and discover how it can be your golden ticket in the freelance world.

The Essence of Personal Branding

At its heart, personal branding is about storytelling. It's the narrative you weave about who you are, what you do, and why it matters. Your personal brand is the emotional and psychological experience people have when they interact with you or your work. It's what people say about you when you're not in the room. A strong personal brand articulates your unique value, your style, and your approach, transforming your professional identity into something memorable and compelling.

Why Personal Branding is Non-Negotiable

In a world teeming with talent, a strong personal brand is what sets you apart. It's the beacon that guides your ideal clients through the noise and straight to your door. But the benefits of personal branding extend far beyond differentiation:

Trust and Credibility: A well-crafted personal brand builds trust and establishes you as an authority in your field. It's a signal to clients that you're not just another freelancer; you're a professional who takes their craft seriously.

Connection and Engagement: Personal branding allows you to connect with your audience on a personal level. By sharing your story, your passions, and your values, you attract clients who resonate with what you stand for, leading to more meaningful and fulfilling collaborations.

Increased Visibility: A strong personal brand amplifies your visibility. Whether through word-of-mouth, social media, or your content, your brand helps you stand out, making it easier for opportunities to find you.

Crafting Your Personal Brand: Where to Begin

Developing a personal brand might seem daunting, but it all starts with introspection:

Identify Your Unique Value Proposition (UVP): What makes you different from the thousands of other freelancers in your field? Is it your unique approach, your background, your specific set of skills? Pinpointing your UVP is the cornerstone of your personal brand.

Define Your Brand Personality: Your brand should reflect your personality. Are you creative and quirky, or are you more serious and analytical? Your brand's tone, language, and visuals should align with who you are, making your brand feel authentic and relatable.

Understand Your Target Audience: Who are you trying to reach? Understanding your ideal clients—their needs, challenges, and aspirations—allows you to tailor your brand messaging to resonate with them deeply.

Communicating Your Brand: The Channels and Tools

With the essence of your brand defined, it's time to bring it to life:

Your Website: Your digital storefront, where your brand story, portfolio, and offerings come together. It's your chance to make a strong, cohesive first impression.

Social Media: Platforms like LinkedIn, Instagram, and Twitter are invaluable for sharing your insights, showcasing your projects, and engaging with your community. Consistency in your visuals and messaging across these platforms reinforces your brand.

Content Creation: Whether it's blogging, podcasting, or video creation, sharing valuable content establishes your expertise and gives your audience a taste of your personality and approach.

Living Your Brand: Authenticity in Action

Personal branding isn't just about what you say; it's about what you do. Living your brand means aligning your actions with your brand values, consistently delivering quality work, and treating every client interaction as an opportunity to reinforce your brand promise. It's about being genuine, reliable, and true to your word, ensuring that the experience of working with you is as remarkable as your brand suggests.

Evolving Your Brand: A Journey, Not a Destination

Your personal brand will grow and evolve with you. As you gain new experiences, develop new skills, and refine your goals, your brand should reflect these changes. Regularly revisiting and updating your brand ensures that it remains relevant and aligned with your current path.

Personal Branding: Your Freelance Superpower

In the end, personal branding is about embracing your uniqueness and sharing it with the world. It's a powerful tool that not only sets you apart but also connects you with the clients and opportunities that are right for you. By crafting a brand that's authentically you, you're not just building a business; you're building a legacy. So dive deep, dream big, and let your personal brand be the beacon that lights your way to freelance success.

Crafting Your Unique Value Proposition: The Key to Standing Out

In the vibrant tapestry of the freelance marketplace, your Unique Value Proposition (UVP) is the thread that makes your brand unmistakably yours. It's the compelling answer to the silent question in every client's mind: "Why should I choose you?" Let's embark on a journey to uncover and articulate your UVP, ensuring that when the right clients come looking, they find not just a freelancer, but a partner who's in a league of their own.

Understanding Your UVP: The Core of Your Freelance Identity

Your UVP is not just a tagline or a catchy phrase; it's the essence of what you bring to the table that nobody else can. It's a blend of your skills, experiences, personality, and the unique way you approach your work. Identifying your UVP requires introspection and a bit of detective work, but it's an investment that pays dividends in clarity, confidence, and clients who are a perfect fit.

Step 1: Dive Deep into Your Skills and Expertise

Begin by laying out all your skills and areas of expertise. But don't stop at the surface level. Dig deeper to uncover the nuances of your knowledge. Perhaps you're a graphic designer with a knack for branding startups, or a copywriter who excels in crafting compelling narratives for non-profits. It's these specifics that start to form the foundation of your UVP.

Step 2: Reflect on Your Unique Experiences and Insights

Your experiences, both professional and personal, shape your perspective and approach to work. Maybe you've traveled extensively, giving you a global perspective that enriches your projects. Or perhaps you've transitioned from another industry, bringing with you insights that offer your clients a fresh angle. These stories and experiences are golden threads in the fabric of your UVP.

Step 3: Identify the Problems You Solve Like No One Else

Think about the challenges and pain points your ideal clients face. Now, consider how your specific blend of skills, experiences, and personal attributes equips you to solve these problems in a way that no one else can. This is where your UVP starts to shine, offering a beacon to clients in search of solutions you're uniquely qualified to provide.

Step 4: Articulate Your UVP with Clarity and Conviction

With your unique blend of skills, experiences, and problem-solving abilities in hand, it's time to craft a statement that encapsulates your UVP. This statement should be clear, concise, and compelling, resonating with your ideal clients and making it evident why you're the perfect choice for their needs. It should speak directly to the benefits they'll receive by working with you, framed in a way that highlights what sets you apart.

Communicating Your UVP: Making Your Mark

With your UVP polished and ready, weaving it into every aspect of your brand communication is crucial. Here's how:

In Your Portfolio: Showcase projects that exemplify your UVP. Use case studies and testimonials to highlight how your unique skills and approach have delivered outstanding results for your clients.

On Your Website and Social Media: Your UVP should be front and center on your website, and echoed across your social media profiles. It's not just about stating your UVP but also demonstrating it through the content you share and the conversations you engage in.

In Your Pitch and Proposals: When reaching out to potential clients or responding to opportunities, tailor your pitch to reflect your UVP. Show them not just what you can do, but how your unique approach aligns with their specific needs and goals.

Living Your UVP: Consistency is Key

The true power of your UVP lies in consistently delivering on its promise. Every project completed, every interaction with clients, and every piece of content you create should reinforce the unique value you offer. This consistency builds trust, cements your reputation, and turns satisfied clients into vocal advocates for your brand.

Your UVP: The Beacon Guiding Your Freelance Journey

Identifying and articulating your UVP is not a one-time exercise but an ongoing process of refinement and evolution. As you grow in your career, gain new experiences, and expand your skills, your UVP will also evolve. Keep it aligned with who you are and the value you deliver, and it will continue to be the beacon that attracts your ideal clients, projects that excite you, and opportunities that propel your freelance career to new heights. Your UVP is not just what makes you different; it's what makes you indispensable.

Chapter 3

Mastering Networking

Welcome to the Art of Connection: Networking in the Freelance World

In the vibrant tapestry of freelancing, the threads that bind success are not just skill and talent but also the connections you weave along the way. Networking—often perceived as a buzzword—is truly an art form in the freelance realm. It's about building bridges, fostering relationships, and creating a supportive community that fuels growth, opportunities, and collaborations. Let's embark on a journey to master the art of networking, transforming it from a daunting task into an enjoyable and fruitful part of your freelance adventure.

The Essence of Networking: It's About Building Relationships

Forget the old image of networking as handing out business cards at stuffy corporate events. In the freelance world, networking is about genuine connections and mutual support. It's about sharing knowledge, offering help, and creating value for others. Approach networking with the mindset of building relationships, not just contacts, and you'll find it becomes a more natural and rewarding part of your professional life.

Crafting Your Networking Strategy: A Personalized Approach

There's no one-size-fits-all strategy for networking; it's about finding what works for you and your unique brand. Some freelancers thrive in online communities, while others prefer face-to-face interactions at local meetups or conferences. The key is to align your networking efforts with your personality, your niche, and your goals. Whether it's joining industry-specific forums, attending workshops, or participating in social media groups, choose platforms and venues where you feel comfortable and where your ideal connections are likely to be.

Leveraging Social Media: The Digital Networking Arena

Social media platforms are a goldmine for freelancers looking to network. LinkedIn, Twitter, Instagram, and even Facebook offer opportunities to connect with peers, mentors, and potential clients. The trick is to be authentic and engaging. Share your work, contribute to conversations, and celebrate the successes of others. Use these platforms to showcase your expertise and your personality, making it clear why someone would want to connect with you.

The Power of Community: Joining Forces with Fellow Freelancers

One of the most overlooked aspects of networking is the potential for collaboration with other freelancers. Instead of viewing your peers as competition, see them as potential partners. Joining or forming a collective of freelancers can open doors to larger projects, shared resources, and new opportunities. Collaborations can also lead to skill swaps, where you exchange services to help each other grow. Remember, a rising tide lifts all boats, and in the freelance community, there's a strong tide of mutual support and collaboration.

The Art of Following Up: Keeping the Connection Alive

Networking isn't just about making initial contact; it's about nurturing those connections over time. Follow up after meetings with a personalized message, keep in touch through social media, and look for opportunities to reconnect, whether it's sharing an article you think they'd like or congratulating them on a recent achievement. Consistent, thoughtful follow-ups keep relationships warm and can turn a casual connection into a valuable ally.

Giving Back: The Secret Ingredient to Networking Success

Perhaps the most powerful networking strategy is to give more than you take. Offer your help, share your expertise, and be a connector for others. Whether it's providing feedback, offering advice, or making introductions, your generosity won't go unnoticed. People remember those who've helped them, and they're often eager to return the favor. This cycle of giving and receiving enriches the entire freelance ecosystem, creating a network of support that's invaluable.

Mastering the Networking Mindset: Embrace the Adventure

Networking can seem intimidating, but when approached with the right mindset, it can be one of the most rewarding aspects of freelancing. See each interaction as an opportunity to learn something new, to be inspired, or to make a difference in someone's journey. Approach networking with curiosity, openness, and a genuine desire to connect, and you'll find that it not only enriches your professional life but also adds depth and meaning to your freelance journey.

Networking: The Lifeline of Your Freelance Career

As you weave your way through the freelance world, remember that networking is much more than a means to an end. It's about community, growth, and the joy of connecting with like-minded individuals. By mastering the art of networking, you're not just building a network; you're building a foundation for a thriving, fulfilling freelance career. So step out with confidence, connect with heart, and watch as your network becomes one of your most treasured assets.

Networking Strategies for Freelancers: Crafting Your Web of Connections

In the kaleidoscopic world of freelancing, your network is more than just a list of contacts—it's a vibrant community that supports, inspires, and opens doors to new possibilities. Effective networking is an art, blending authenticity with strategy, to weave a web of connections that grows with your career. Let's explore the strategies that can help you build and expand your professional network, making every interaction count.

Embrace Your Story: The Heart of Authentic Connections

Your journey, with its unique blend of experiences, challenges, and triumphs, is your most potent networking tool. Embracing and sharing your story not only makes you relatable but also memorable. Whether it's through a blog post, a social media update, or a conversation at a networking event, let your authentic self shine through. People connect with people, not resumes, and your story is the bridge that turns a professional interaction into a meaningful relationship.

Diversify Your Networking Arenas: Beyond the Conventional

While industry events and conferences are traditional networking hubs, don't limit yourself to these alone. Look for opportunities in less conventional settings, such as workshops, online forums, social media groups, and even local community events. Each arena offers a unique chance to connect with others in a more relaxed and authentic way. Remember, valuable connections can happen anywhere, from a Twitter chat to a local art show.

Leverage Social Media with Purpose: Your Digital Handshake

Social media is a powerful tool for freelancers to network, but it's not just about being present—it's about engaging with purpose. Choose platforms that align with your industry and where your ideal connections are active. Use these platforms to showcase your work, share insights, and contribute to discussions. Engage with others' content thoughtfully, offering genuine comments and insights. Think of social media interactions as digital handshakes, each one an opportunity to introduce yourself and make a lasting impression.

Cultivate Relationships with Thought Leaders and Influencers

Connecting with thought leaders and influencers in your field can be incredibly rewarding. Start by engaging with their content—share their articles, comment on their posts, and participate in discussions they're leading. Over time, as you contribute valuable insights, you'll become a familiar presence. This can open the door to more direct interactions, collaborations, and even mentorship opportunities. Remember, the goal is not to seek immediate gain but to build genuine relationships that are mutually beneficial.

Offer Value First: The Golden Rule of Networking

The golden rule of networking is to offer value before you ask for anything. Whether it's sharing a helpful resource, offering a solution to a problem, or simply providing a listening ear, your willingness to help others creates goodwill and establishes you as a valuable member of your community. This approach not only enriches your relationships but often leads to unexpected opportunities and collaborations.

Master the Art of Follow-Up: Keeping the Connection Alive

The initial connection is just the beginning. The art of networking lies in the follow-up. After meeting someone new, whether online or in person, reach out with a personalized message. Mention something specific from your interaction to jog their memory and express your interest in staying in touch. Regular, non-intrusive follow-ups keep the relationship warm, turning casual contacts into meaningful connections.

Engage in Collaborative Projects: Networking through Creation

One of the most effective ways to network is by collaborating on projects. Collaborations allow you to showcase your skills, learn from others, and create something that's greater than the sum of its parts. Whether it's a joint article, a webinar, or a community project, collaborative efforts not only expand your network but also enhance your portfolio.

Be an Active Participant in Communities: Your Networking Ecosystem

Whether it's an online forum, a professional organization, or a social media group, actively participating in communities related to your field is invaluable. Don't just lurk—contribute. Answer questions, share resources, and support others' successes. Over time, your active participation establishes you as a trusted and helpful member of the community, leading to deeper connections and more opportunities.

Networking: A Journey of Connection and Growth

As you weave your web of connections, remember that networking is a journey, not a destination. It's about growing alongside your peers, discovering new opportunities, and contributing to the fabric of your industry. Approach networking with openness, generosity, and a dash of courage, and watch as your professional network becomes a cornerstone of your freelance success.

Leveraging Social Media: Navigating the Digital Networking Landscape

In the ever-evolving digital age, social media stands as a beacon for freelancers, illuminating pathways to connect, engage, and grow in ways previously unimaginable. Platforms like LinkedIn, Twitter, and Instagram are not just tools for socializing but powerful engines for networking, brand building, and forging meaningful connections with peers and potential clients. Let's delve into the art of leveraging these platforms to expand your professional network and open doors to new opportunities.

LinkedIn: The Professional Networking Powerhouse

LinkedIn is the cornerstone of professional networking online, a virtual meeting room where freelancers can connect with industry leaders, peers, and potential clients. Here's how to make the most of it:

Optimize Your Profile: Your LinkedIn profile is your digital resume and portfolio rolled into one. Ensure it's fully optimized by including a professional photo, a compelling headline, a detailed summary that highlights your UVP, and a comprehensive listing of your skills and experiences.

Showcase Your Work: Use the featured section to showcase your best work, be it articles you've written, projects you've completed, or testimonials from satisfied clients. This not only highlights your expertise but also gives potential clients a taste of what you can offer.

Engage and Contribute: Regularly share insights, industry news, and updates on your projects. Comment thoughtfully on others' posts and participate in relevant groups. This consistent engagement positions you as an active and knowledgeable member of your industry.

Twitter: The Pulse of Industry Conversations

Twitter's fast-paced, conversational nature makes it an excellent platform for freelancers to stay on top of industry trends, join real-time discussions, and connect with a broader audience.

Curate Your Feed: Follow industry leaders, influencers, and potential clients in your niche. Their tweets can provide valuable insights and opportunities to engage.

Join the Conversation: Participate in industry-related Twitter chats, use relevant hashtags, and don't shy away from starting discussions. Your tweets can attract attention from potential clients and collaborators who value your insights.

Share Valuable Content: Regularly tweet and retweet content that is valuable to your audience. This can include tips, articles, and insights related to your field, as well as updates on your own work and achievements.

Instagram: Visual Storytelling Meets Networking

For freelancers whose work has a strong visual component, Instagram offers a unique platform to showcase their portfolio and connect with clients and peers through the power of visual storytelling.

Build Your Brand Aesthetically: Ensure your Instagram feed reflects your personal brand, with a consistent style and theme that showcases your work and personality.

Use Stories and Reels: Instagram Stories and Reels offer dynamic ways to share behind-the-scenes glimpses, work-in-progress shots, and personal insights, adding depth to your professional persona.

Engage with Your Community: Comment on posts by peers and potential clients, respond to comments on your own posts, and use Instagram's DM feature for more personal interactions. Engaging with your community fosters relationships and keeps you top of mind.

Cross-Platform Strategies: Amplifying Your Presence

While each platform has its unique strengths, using them in tandem can amplify your networking efforts.

Cross-Promote Your Content: Share your Instagram posts on Twitter, link your latest blog post on LinkedIn, and cross-promote content across platforms to reach a wider audience.

Consistent Branding Across Platforms: Ensure your branding, from your profile pictures to your bio descriptions, is consistent across all platforms. This coherence strengthens your personal brand and makes you easily recognizable.

Leverage Analytics: Use the analytics tools provided by these platforms to understand which types of content resonate with your audience, the best times to post, and how to improve your engagement rates.

Social Media: The Gateway to Global Connections

In leveraging social media for networking, the key is to be authentic, provide value, and engage genuinely. These platforms offer a global stage to showcase your talents, share your journey, and connect with like-minded individuals and potential clients from all corners of the world. By strategically navigating the digital networking landscape, you can transform social media from a casual interaction space into a powerful catalyst for your freelance career growth.

Chapter 4

Monetizing Your Skills

Turning Passion into Paychecks: The Freelancer's Guide to Monetizing Skills

In the colorful mosaic of freelancing, each skill you possess is akin to a unique tile, capable of creating a masterpiece of a career when placed with intention and strategy. Monetizing your skills is not merely about making ends meet; it's about crafting a fulfilling career that aligns with your passions and lifestyle. Let's navigate the path to transforming your talents into tangible rewards, ensuring that every stroke of your work contributes to the grand canvas of your professional life.

Identifying Marketable Skills: Your Freelance Arsenal

The first step in monetizing your skills is identifying which of them are in demand. Dive deep into your repertoire and distinguish between hobbies, passions, and marketable skills. Not every interest needs to become a revenue stream, but understanding the market value of your skills is crucial. Conduct research within your industry, observe trends, and listen to the needs of potential clients to pinpoint which of your skills can solve real-world problems.

Packaging Your Services: Crafting Irresistible Offers

Once you've identified your marketable skills, the next challenge is packaging them into compelling services. This involves more than listing what you can do; it's about framing your services in a way that highlights the benefits to your clients. For instance, if you're a graphic designer, don't just offer logo design; present a brand identity package that promises to elevate your client's market presence. Packaging your services effectively makes them more attractive and easier for clients to understand the value they're getting.

Setting the Right Rates: Valuing Your Work

One of the most daunting aspects of freelancing is determining what to charge for your services. Set your rates too low, and you might undervalue your work; set them too high, and you risk alienating potential clients. Consider factors like your experience, the complexity of the work, industry standards, and the value you bring to the table. Don't be afraid to start with a rate that feels right and adjust as you gain more insight and experience. Remember, your rates should reflect not just the time you spend but also the expertise and value you offer.

Finding Your Niche: The Sweet Spot of Demand and Passion

In a sea of freelancers, finding a niche can help you stand out and attract the right clients. Your niche should be at the intersection of what you're passionate about, what you're good at, and what the market needs. Specializing allows you to hone your skills further, command higher rates, and become the go-to expert in your area. Whether it's copywriting for eco-friendly brands or web development for e-commerce sites, finding your niche makes your marketing efforts more targeted and effective.

Building an Online Presence: Your Digital Storefront

In today's digital age, having a strong online presence is non-negotiable for freelancers looking to monetize their skills. Your website should showcase your portfolio, highlight your services, and make it easy for clients to contact you. Use social media to share your work, engage with your audience, and build your brand. An online presence not only increases your visibility but also adds credibility to your freelance business.

Leveraging Platforms and Marketplaces: Connecting with Clients

Platforms like Upwork, Freelancer, and Fiverr can be valuable resources for finding clients, especially when you're starting. While they may take a commission, these platforms offer the opportunity to build your portfolio, gain experience, and secure testimonials. As you grow, you can transition to securing clients through your network and online presence, where you have more control over your rates and client relationships.

Mastering the Art of Pitching: Selling Your Services

Monetizing your skills involves not just having talent but also being able to sell that talent. Crafting compelling pitches and proposals is crucial in convincing potential clients of the value you offer. Tailor each pitch to the client's specific needs, highlighting how your skills can solve their problems and contribute to their goals. A well-crafted pitch can make the difference between a prospective client passing you by and one who's eager to work with you.

Continuous Learning and Upskilling: Staying Ahead of the Curve

The freelance landscape is ever-evolving, and staying relevant means committing to continuous learning. Investing in your professional development not only enhances your current service offerings but also allows you to expand into new areas. Attend workshops, take online courses, and stay abreast of industry trends. Upskilling is a surefire way to add value to your services, attract a broader client base, and justify higher rates.

Monetizing Your Skills: A Journey of Growth and Empowerment

Transforming your skills into a thriving freelance career is a journey marked by growth, learning, and adaptability. By identifying and packaging your services, setting the right rates, finding your niche, and continuously enhancing your skills, you're not just monetizing your talents; you're building a career that's rewarding both professionally and personally. Embrace the journey, for every skill you monetize brings you one step closer to the freelance career of your dreams.

Finding Your Niche: Carving Out Your Unique Space in the Freelance World

In the sprawling garden of freelancing, finding your niche is akin to discovering a fertile patch of soil where your particular skills can bloom most vibrantly. It's about aligning your passions and proficiencies with the needs of the market, creating a harmonious blend that not only fulfills you but also serves a specific audience. Let's embark on a journey to unearth your niche, ensuring that your freelance career is not just fruitful but also deeply rewarding.

The Essence of a Niche: More Than Just Specialization

A common misconception is that finding a niche means narrowing your focus to a single skill or service. While specialization is a component, a true niche encompasses understanding the specific problems you solve, for whom you solve them, and the unique way in which you approach these solutions. It's the intersection of your expertise, your passions, and market demand that forms the sweet spot of your niche.

Self-Reflection: Unearthing Your Passions and Strengths

The quest for your niche begins with introspection. Dive into your skills and interests with an open heart. What tasks do you find most fulfilling? In which projects do you excel, and receive the most praise? Sometimes, your niche finds you through the patterns in your work that bring you the most joy and recognition. Remember, your niche should not only be profitable but should also resonate with your core interests and values.

Market Research: Identifying Opportunities and Needs

With a clearer understanding of your passions and strengths, turn your gaze outward to the market. Who needs the skills you offer? What specific problems are they facing that you can solve? Conduct market research by exploring industry forums, social media groups, and online platforms where your potential clients gather. Look for recurring themes in their discussions and challenges; these are potential niches begging for your expertise.

Analyzing the Competition: Finding Your Unique Angle

Understanding your competition is crucial in carving out your niche. Who else is offering similar services, and how can you differentiate yourself? Maybe you bring a unique perspective from your background, or perhaps you combine skills in a way that no one else does. Your unique angle isn't just about being different; it's about adding distinctive value that sets you apart from the crowd.

Testing the Waters: Validating Your Niche

Before fully committing to a niche, test its viability. Offer a pilot service, create a mini-project, or conduct a survey within your target market. This preliminary exploration not only provides insight into the demand for your services but also allows you to refine your approach based on real feedback. Remember, the goal is to find a niche where your skills are not just appreciated but sought after.

Crafting Your Value Proposition: Communicating Your Niche

Once you've identified and validated your niche, articulate your value proposition clearly. What exactly can you offer to your niche market that no one else can? This value proposition should encapsulate the unique benefits your clients will receive by choosing you. Whether it's through your website, social media profiles, or direct pitches, ensure that your messaging resonates with your target audience and highlights your niche expertise.

Building Authority: Establishing Yourself as the Go-To Expert

With your niche and value proposition defined, focus on building authority within your space. Share your knowledge through blog posts, social media content, webinars, or speaking engagements. Engaging with your community not only reinforces your expertise but also strengthens your network within your niche, leading to more opportunities and referrals.

Adapting and Evolving: Keeping Your Niche Fresh

The freelance landscape is dynamic, with market needs and opportunities constantly evolving. Keep your finger on the pulse of your niche, staying attuned to shifts in demand, emerging trends, and new challenges your clients face. Being adaptable allows you to evolve your niche over time, ensuring that your services remain relevant and in demand.

Finding Your Niche: A Journey to the Heart of Your Freelance Career

Finding your niche is a journey of exploration, both inward into your passions and skills, and outward into the needs of the market. It's about finding that sweet spot where what you love to do meets what others need and are willing to pay for. By identifying, validating, and communicating your niche, you're not just carving out a space in the freelance world; you're building a foundation for a career that's not only profitable but profoundly satisfying. Embrace the journey, for in finding your niche, you find the key to unlocking the full potential of your freelance career.

Setting Rates and Negotiating Contracts: Navigating the Freelance Financial Seas

In the grand adventure of freelancing, setting your rates and negotiating contracts are akin to setting the sails on your ship, guiding you through calm and stormy waters alike towards financial success and client satisfaction. This journey is not just about numbers; it's about recognizing your worth, understanding the market, and communicating your value effectively. Let's chart a course through the intricacies of pricing and negotiation, ensuring that your freelance voyage is both prosperous and fulfilling.

Understanding Your Value: The Foundation of Your Rates

Before you can set your rates, you must first understand the value you bring to the table. This isn't just about the time you spend on a project but the expertise, unique perspective, and solutions you provide. Consider factors such as your experience, the complexity of your services, the results you deliver, and the going rate in your industry. Remember, your rates are a reflection of your value, not just your time.

Market Research: Gauging the Freelance Waters

Embark on a reconnaissance mission to understand the pricing landscape in your field. Explore platforms where similar services are offered, connect with peers in your industry, and consider joining professional associations to gain insights. This research will help you establish a baseline, ensuring your rates are competitive yet fair, striking the right balance between affordability for clients and sustainability for you.

Pricing Strategies: Charting Your Course

There are several strategies you can employ when setting your rates:

Hourly Rates: Ideal for projects where the scope is flexible or hard to define upfront. This method ensures you're compensated for every hour worked but requires diligent time tracking.

Project-Based Rates: Suited for projects with a clear scope and deliverables, allowing you to quote a fixed price. This can be more appealing to clients as it provides cost certainty.

Value-Based Pricing: This approach involves pricing based on the value or outcome your work provides to the client, potentially allowing for higher rates but requiring a deep understanding of your client's business and goals.

Choose the strategy that aligns with your services, your work style, and your clients' preferences, and be open to adapting as needed.

Communicating Your Rates: The Art of Transparency

When discussing rates with potential clients, clarity and confidence are key. Be transparent about what your rates include and the value clients can expect to receive. Prepare to articulate why you're worth your rates, using past results, testimonials, or case studies. Remember, the way you present your rates often sets the tone for how clients perceive your value.

Negotiating Contracts: Navigating the Negotiation Seas

Negotiation is a natural part of the freelancing journey. Approach these discussions with a collaborative mindset, aiming for a win-win outcome where both you and the client feel valued and satisfied.

Know Your Boundaries: Before entering negotiations, know your minimum acceptable rate and the conditions you're willing to work under. This clarity will help you navigate negotiations without compromising too much.

Focus on Value, Not Just Price: If a client balks at your rates, steer the conversation towards the value and results you provide, not just the cost. Highlight how your work can solve their problems or contribute to their goals.

Be Open to Creative Solutions: Sometimes, meeting in the middle isn't just about lowering your rate. Consider other value adds or adjustments to the project scope that can make the contract work for both parties.

Adjusting Your Sails: Review and Adapt Your Rates Regularly

The freelance market is dynamic, and your rates should be too. Regularly review and adjust your rates in response to changes in your experience level, the complexity of your services, and market demand. Annual reviews or adjustments in line with significant skill upgrades or portfolio expansions are good practices.

Contracts: Your Freelance Compass

A well-crafted contract is not just a formality; it's a crucial tool that outlines the scope of work, deliverables, timelines, payment terms, and other conditions of your engagement. It sets clear expectations, mitigates misunderstandings, and provides a legal safeguard for both parties. Ensure your contracts are clear, comprehensive, and reflect the agreed-upon terms, including any negotiations.

Setting Rates and Negotiating Contracts: The Freelancer's Voyage to Value

Mastering the art of setting rates and negotiating contracts is a crucial skill on your freelance journey. It's about more than just numbers; it's about understanding your worth, communicating your value, and crafting agreements that support your career's growth and sustainability. With each negotiation, you're not just earning your worth; you're affirming the value of your work and paving the way for a successful freelance future.

Chapter 5

Managing Your Freelance Business

Steering Your Freelance Ship: Mastering the Art of Business Management

In the vast ocean of freelancing, where the waters are as unpredictable as they are exciting, managing your freelance business is akin to being the captain of your own ship. It's not just about navigating through client projects but also about charting a course for your business's growth, sustainability, and resilience. Let's embark on a journey to explore the essential skills and tools you need to steer your freelance venture towards success.

Organizational Mastery: Keeping Your Deck in Order

The backbone of any successful freelance business is organization. With multiple projects, deadlines, and client communications to juggle, developing a system to keep everything in order is crucial.

Project Management Tools: Leverage digital tools like Trello, Asana, or Notion to track your projects, deadlines, and tasks. These platforms allow you to visualize your workload, prioritize tasks, and ensure nothing falls through the cracks.

Time Management Techniques: Adopt time management methodologies that resonate with your working style, whether it's the Pomodoro Technique, time blocking, or the Eisenhower Matrix. Remember, in freelancing, time is not just money; it's also your freedom and well-being.

Financial Navigation: Charting Your Financial Course

Managing your finances with precision is vital in the unpredictable waters of freelancing. A sound financial strategy ensures your business remains viable and your personal livelihood is secure.

Budgeting and Forecasting: Develop a budget that covers your business expenses, taxes, and personal salary. Use forecasting to anticipate slow periods and plan accordingly, ensuring financial stability.

Invoicing and Payments: Utilize invoicing software like FreshBooks or QuickBooks to streamline your billing process. Clearly state payment terms to avoid delays, and consider using online payment platforms to make transactions smoother for your clients.

Saving for the Future: Set aside a portion of your income for retirement and emergencies. Freelancing offers freedom, but it also requires you to be your own safety net.

Client Relations: Nurturing Your Crew and Passengers

Your clients are the lifeblood of your freelance business, and nurturing these relationships is key to ongoing success.

Communication: Maintain open, clear, and professional communication with your clients. Regular updates, asking for feedback, and being responsive build trust and rapport.

Setting Boundaries: Clearly define your availability, scope of work, and revision policies from the outset. Setting boundaries protects your time and energy, ensuring you can deliver your best work.

Client Onboarding and Offboarding: Develop a streamlined process for bringing new clients onboard and closing projects. This not only enhances the client experience but also sets the stage for future collaborations or referrals.

Marketing and Branding: Sailing with Your Flags High

In a sea of freelancers, your marketing and branding efforts are your flags, signaling your presence and attracting the right kind of attention.

Consistent Branding: Ensure your brand is consistent across all platforms, from your website to your social media profiles. A cohesive brand strengthens your professional image and makes you more memorable.

Content Marketing: Share valuable content related to your niche through blogs, social media, or a newsletter. Content marketing establishes your expertise and can attract potential clients.

Networking: Continuous networking, both online and offline, keeps you connected to industry trends, potential clients, and collaboration opportunities. Remember, your next big project could come from a connection made today.

Continuous Learning and Adaptation: Evolving with the Tides

The freelance landscape is ever-changing, and staying adaptable and committed to continuous learning ensures you can navigate through any storm.

Skill Development: Regularly invest in upgrading your skills and expanding your offerings. Online courses, webinars, and workshops are great ways to keep learning.

Industry Trends: Stay abreast of trends and changes in your industry. Being knowledgeable makes you a valuable resource to your clients and helps you adapt your services to meet evolving needs.

Managing Your Freelance Business: The Captain's Endeavor

Managing your freelance business is a multifaceted endeavor, requiring you to wear multiple hats and juggle various responsibilities. From organizational prowess and financial acumen to nurturing client relationships and marketing your brand, each aspect is a crucial gear in the machinery of your freelance success. Remember, at the helm of your freelance ship, you have the power to steer your business towards uncharted territories of opportunity and growth. Embrace the journey, for it's not just about the destinations you reach but the captain you become along the way.

Project Management for Freelancers: Orchestrating Your Symphony of Tasks

In the grand orchestra of freelancing, managing multiple projects is akin to conducting a symphony, where each task is an instrumentalist waiting for your cue. The harmony of your freelance career relies on your ability to orchestrate these elements seamlessly, ensuring that every project reaches its crescendo without missing a beat. Let's delve into the tools and techniques that can help you master the art of project management, turning potential chaos into a well-composed masterpiece.

The Blueprint of Project Management: Understanding the Fundamentals

Project management, at its core, is about clarity, organization, and adaptability. It involves setting clear goals, prioritizing tasks, tracking progress, and adjusting as needed. The goal is to complete projects efficiently and effectively, satisfying clients while maintaining your sanity and work-life balance.

Selecting Your Instruments: Choosing the Right Project Management Tools

In the digital age, freelancers have a plethora of tools at their disposal, each with its unique features designed to simplify project management. Here's how to select the right ones for your ensemble:

Task Management Tools: Platforms like Asana, Trello, and Notion allow you to create tasks, assign deadlines, and track progress visually. Choose a tool that resonates with your workflow, whether you prefer a kanban board, a list, or a calendar view.

Time Tracking Software: Tools like Harvest, Toggl, and RescueTime not only help you keep track of the hours spent on each project but also provide insights into your productivity patterns, enabling you to optimize your work habits.

Collaboration Platforms: If your projects involve working with clients or other freelancers, consider using collaboration tools like Slack or Microsoft Teams to streamline communication and file sharing, keeping everyone in tune.

Composing Your Workflow: Setting Up Efficient Processes

An efficient workflow is the backbone of effective project management. Here's how to structure yours:

Start with a Clear Brief: Every project should begin with a clear brief that outlines the scope, objectives, deadlines, and any other critical information. This serves as the score sheet for your symphony, guiding every move.

Break It Down: Divide each project into smaller, manageable tasks. Assign deadlines and priorities to each task, turning the overwhelming into the achievable.

Batching and Time Blocking: Group similar tasks together and allocate specific blocks of time to focus on them. This technique reduces context switching and increases efficiency, allowing you to immerse fully in each task set.

Conducting the Orchestra: Managing Tasks and Deadlines

With your tools selected and workflow set, it's time to lead your orchestra. Here's how to ensure every section plays in harmony:

Daily and Weekly Planning: Start each day and week with a plan. Review your tasks and deadlines, and set clear goals for what you aim to achieve. This planning session is your moment to direct the focus of your ensemble.

Use Milestones: For larger projects, set milestones to mark significant progress points. Milestones act as checkpoints, allowing you to assess progress and adjust your strategy if needed.

Stay Agile: Flexibility is key in freelancing. Be prepared to adjust your plans as projects evolve, new tasks arise, or unexpected challenges occur. An agile approach ensures you can adapt without losing your rhythm.

The Art of Prioritization: Playing the Right Notes at the Right Time

Not all tasks are created equal. Prioritizing ensures that you focus on what's most critical at any given moment.

The Eisenhower Matrix: Use this tool to categorize tasks into urgent, important, both, or neither. This helps you focus on tasks that are both urgent and important, preventing last-minute rushes and stress.

The 80/20 Rule: Remember that 80% of your results often come from 20% of your efforts. Identify tasks that have the most significant impact and allocate your time and energy accordingly.

Intermissions and Encores: The Importance of Breaks and Reflection

Just as a symphony has intermissions, your workday should include breaks to rest and recharge. Regular pauses enhance creativity and prevent burnout. Additionally, after completing each project, take time to reflect on what went well and what could be improved. This reflection is your encore, setting the stage for even better performances in the future.

Project Management for Freelancers: Your Symphony of Success

Mastering project management is about more than just keeping track of tasks and deadlines; it's about orchestrating a workflow that allows you to deliver exceptional work, satisfy your clients, and enjoy the freelance lifestyle. With the right tools, techniques, and a conductor's keen sense of timing and adaptability, you can turn the potential cacophony of managing multiple projects into a harmonious symphony of success.

Financial Management: Navigating the Freelancer's Fiscal Waters

In the vast expanse of freelancing, adept financial management is akin to mastering the art of navigation in uncharted waters. It's the skill that ensures not only your survival but your prosperity in the fluctuating tides of freelance income. Budgeting, invoicing, and taxes are the sextant, compass, and map guiding you through fiscal uncertainties to the safe harbors of financial stability and growth. Let's embark on a journey to demystify these essentials, turning the daunting into the doable.

Budgeting: Charting Your Financial Course

Budgeting is the cornerstone of effective financial management, providing a clear view of your income, expenses, and savings goals. It's about understanding the flow of your financial currents and steering your resources towards your priorities.

Track Your Income and Expenses: Begin by tracking every penny that comes in and goes out. This will give you a clear picture of your financial health and help identify areas where adjustments might be needed.

Separate Personal and Business Finances: Use separate bank accounts for your personal and business finances. This separation simplifies bookkeeping, tax preparation, and gives you a clearer picture of your business's financial performance.

Plan for Irregular Income: Freelancing income can ebb and flow. Create a budget that accommodates this variability, including a buffer for leaner months and a strategy for saving during more bountiful times.

Set Financial Goals: Whether it's saving for a new piece of equipment, a professional development course, or an emergency fund, setting clear financial goals gives your budget direction and purpose.

Invoicing: The Art of Claiming Your Worth

Invoicing isn't just a formality; it's the lifeline of your cash flow, the rhythm by which your freelance business pulses. Mastering the art of invoicing ensures that this rhythm remains steady and strong.

Use Professional Invoicing Software: Platforms like FreshBooks, QuickBooks, or Wave offer professional invoicing templates, automate reminders for overdue payments, and streamline the payment process for your clients.

Be Clear and Detailed: Ensure your invoices are clear, detailed, and include all necessary information: your contact details, services provided, payment terms, due date, and payment methods.

Establish Payment Terms Upfront: Discuss and agree upon payment terms with your clients before starting a project. Whether it's net 30, net 60, or upon delivery, clear terms prevent misunderstandings and delays.

Follow Up on Late Payments: Don't shy away from following up on overdue invoices. A polite reminder often suffices, but don't hesitate to enforce your agreed-upon terms if necessary.

Taxes: Navigating the Freelancer's Fiscal Maze

Taxes can seem like a daunting labyrinth, but with the right knowledge and preparation, you can navigate them with confidence, ensuring you meet your obligations without overpaying.

Understand Your Tax Responsibilities: Familiarize yourself with the tax requirements for freelancers in your jurisdiction, including income tax, self-employment tax, and any other applicable taxes.

Save for Taxes: Set aside a portion of each payment for taxes. Keeping this in a separate savings account helps ensure that you're prepared when tax payments are due.

Track Expenses Religiously: Keep meticulous records of all business-related expenses. These can often be deducted from your taxable income, lowering your tax liability. Consider using a digital tool or app to simplify this process.

Consider Professional Help: Taxes can be complex, and the cost of a mistake high. Investing in the services of a tax professional or accountant can save you time, stress, and potentially money in the long run.

Financial Management: The Freelancer's Fiscal Compass

Effective financial management is more than a set of tasks; it's a mindset that values foresight, organization, and proactive planning. By mastering budgeting, you ensure your freelance ship remains buoyant even in uncertain waters. Through proficient invoicing, you maintain the rhythm of your cash flow, fueling your journey forward. And by adeptly navigating your tax responsibilities, you safeguard your voyage from potential pitfalls. Together, these practices form the compass that guides you towards financial security and success in the freelancing world, allowing you to focus on what you do best: your craft.

Chapter 6

Growing Your Career

Embarking on the Voyage of Career Growth in Freelancing

In the boundless realm of freelancing, growth is not merely an aspiration but a necessity, the very wind that propels your vessel forward into new and uncharted territories. This journey of career growth is a mosaic of continuous learning, strategic positioning, and the cultivation of meaningful relationships. It's about expanding your horizons, elevating your craft, and navigating towards increasingly rewarding opportunities. Let's set sail and explore the strategies that will guide your freelance career to new heights and horizons.

Continuous Learning: Charting a Course for Mastery

In the ever-evolving landscape of freelancing, the thirst for knowledge and the pursuit of mastery are your compass and sextant, guiding you through the shifting currents of industry trends and technological advancements.

Skill Enhancement: Dedicate time to refining your existing skills and acquiring new ones. Online courses, webinars, workshops, and conferences are treasure troves of knowledge, waiting to be discovered.

Industry Trends: Stay abreast of the latest trends and innovations in your field. Subscribe to industry newsletters, follow thought leaders on social media, and engage with professional communities to keep your knowledge fresh and relevant.

Diversification: Consider expanding your service offerings by exploring complementary skills or niches. Diversification not only makes you more adaptable but also opens up new streams of income.

Strategic Positioning: Navigating Towards Your Ideal Market

Understanding your market and positioning yourself strategically within it is akin to setting your sails to catch the most favorable winds, ensuring a smooth and efficient journey towards your desired destination.

Define Your Ideal Client: Who do you enjoy working with the most? What types of projects fuel your passion and bring out your best work? Defining your ideal client helps you tailor your marketing efforts and service offerings to attract more of these rewarding collaborations.

Personal Branding: Cultivate a strong personal brand that resonates with your target audience. Your brand is your flag, signaling your presence and expertise to potential clients and collaborators.

Value Proposition: Hone your unique value proposition. Clearly articulating the unique benefits you provide sets you apart in a crowded marketplace and makes you the go-to expert in your niche.

Networking and Collaboration: Building Your Fleet of Allies

In the vast ocean of freelancing, no one is an island. Building a network of allies, collaborators, and mentors is like assembling a fleet, providing support, guidance, and companionship on your journey.

Cultivate Meaningful Relationships: Engage with your peers, clients, and industry leaders with genuine interest and generosity. Offer help without immediate expectation of return, and you'll build a network of support that's both rewarding and resilient.

Collaborate: Seek opportunities for collaboration, whether on client projects, joint ventures, or community initiatives. Collaborations can expand your skill set, expose you to new audiences, and lead to innovative ideas and solutions.

Mentorship: Find a mentor who can guide you through the complexities of freelancing and career growth. Similarly, consider mentoring others. Teaching is a powerful way to consolidate your own knowledge and give back to the community.

Personal Development: The Inner Journey of Growth

While skills, positioning, and networking are crucial, true growth also involves an inward journey, nurturing the qualities that sustain you through the challenges and triumphs of freelancing.

Resilience: Cultivate resilience to navigate through setbacks and failures. View every challenge as an opportunity to learn and grow stronger.

Adaptability: Embrace change and be willing to pivot when necessary. The freelance landscape is dynamic, and adaptability is key to thriving amidst uncertainty.

Well-being: Prioritize your physical and mental health. Sustainable career growth is built on a foundation of well-being, allowing you to perform at your best over the long term.

Growing Your Career: Charting the Path to New Horizons

Growing your freelance career is a voyage that spans the breadth of skill mastery, strategic positioning, and deep personal development. It's about embracing the journey with curiosity, courage, and an open heart, ready to learn from every experience and interaction. By committing to continuous growth, nurturing meaningful relationships, and staying true to your course, you'll not only achieve success but also find fulfillment and joy in the adventure of freelancing. The horizon is vast, and the possibilities are endless. Set your sights high, for in the world of freelancing, the only limits are those you set for yourself.

Continuous Learning and Skill Development

Charting the Course for Endless Horizons

In the vast expanse of the freelancing universe, continuous learning and skill development are the guiding stars that illuminate the path to uncharted territories of opportunity and success. Just as a ship's captain must navigate ever-changing seas, a freelancer must navigate the ever-evolving landscape of their industry. This journey of perpetual growth is not just about staying afloat but about sailing towards new horizons with confidence and prowess.

Embracing the Winds of Change: The Imperative of Continuous Learning

The only constant in the freelancing world is change. New technologies emerge, industry standards evolve, and client needs shift. Staying updated with these changes is not merely beneficial—it's imperative for survival and growth. Continuous learning ensures that your skills remain relevant and competitive, enabling you to meet and exceed the expectations of your clients and the industry at large.

Stay Informed: Make it a habit to stay informed about the latest trends and developments in your field. Subscribe to industry newsletters, follow thought leaders on social media, and participate in relevant forums and discussions. This constant influx of new information keeps your knowledge base fresh and your perspective innovative.

Expand Your Skill Set: The breadth of your skills can significantly impact the scope of opportunities available to you. Actively seek to expand your skill set by learning new tools, technologies, and methodologies. Online platforms like Udemy, Coursera, and LinkedIn Learning offer a plethora of courses that cater to virtually every skill and interest.

Specialize and Diversify: While deepening your expertise in a specific area can make you a sought-after specialist, diversifying your skills can open up new avenues for work and collaboration. Striking a balance between specialization and diversification can make your freelance business more resilient and adaptable to market changes.

The Art of Skill Application: Beyond Acquisition

Acquiring new skills is only the first step; the true art lies in their application. Every new skill or piece of knowledge you gain should be integrated into your work, enhancing the quality and range of your services.

Practical Projects: Apply new skills to practical projects as soon as possible. Whether it's a personal project, a pro bono work, or a small component of a larger client project, real-world application cements learning and boosts confidence.

Showcase Your Growth: Update your portfolio, resume, and professional profiles to reflect your newly acquired skills and competencies. This not only demonstrates your commitment to growth but also increases your attractiveness to potential clients.

Feedback and Reflection: Seek feedback on your work, especially when it involves newly acquired skills. Reflect on this feedback and use it as a basis for further learning and improvement.

Networking and Collaborative Learning: Sailing Together

The journey of continuous learning is not a solitary voyage. Engaging with a community of peers, mentors, and collaborators can significantly enhance the learning experience, providing insights, encouragement, and opportunities to learn from others.

Professional Communities: Join professional communities, both online and offline, related to your field. These communities can be invaluable sources of support, knowledge exchange, and professional opportunities.

Mentorship and Coaching: Seek out mentors or coaches who can guide your learning journey, offer valuable insights, and challenge you to grow beyond your comfort zones. Conversely, mentoring others can also deepen your understanding and reinforce your own learning.

Collaboration: Collaborate with other freelancers or professionals on projects that push you to apply and expand your skills. Collaboration not only leads to skill enhancement but also opens up new perspectives and approaches to problem-solving.

Continuous Learning: The Freelancer's Lifelong Quest

In the realm of freelancing, continuous learning and skill development are not just strategies for career advancement; they are the very essence of professional vitality and creativity. They fuel your ability to innovate, adapt, and thrive in an ever-changing landscape. By committing to lifelong learning, you not only ensure your relevance but also enhance your capacity for personal and professional fulfillment. The horizon of knowledge is boundless, and each new skill is a beacon leading you to greater heights. Embrace this journey with enthusiasm and an open mind, for in the world of freelancing, growth is both the journey and the destination.

Scaling Your Freelance Business

In the adventurous voyage of freelancing, scaling your business is akin to discovering new continents, expanding your territory beyond the familiar shores of individual projects into the vast seas of greater opportunities and challenges. It's a journey that requires not just hard work and dedication but strategic planning, delegation, and a strong personal brand that acts as your flagship. Let's navigate through the strategies that can propel your freelance business to new heights, transforming it from a solo endeavor into a thriving enterprise.

Laying the Keel: Foundations of Scaling

Before you set sail on the expansion journey, it's crucial to strengthen the keel of your business—the fundamental systems and processes that support growth. This includes streamlining your workflow, automating repetitive tasks, and ensuring your financial management is robust and scalable. Investing time and resources in solidifying these foundations ensures your business can withstand the challenges of scaling.

Outsourcing and Delegation: Building Your Crew

As a freelancer, your capacity for growth is inherently limited by the number of hours in a day. To transcend this limitation, consider outsourcing or delegating tasks that fall outside your core competencies or consume excessive time.

Identify Delegable Tasks: Audit your workflow to identify tasks that can be outsourced, such as administrative duties, social media management, or even certain aspects of your client work.

Hiring Freelancers or Contractors: Collaborate with other freelancers or hire contractors to take on tasks that can be done more efficiently or effectively by others. This not only frees up your time for higher-value work but also brings new skills and perspectives to your business.

Maintaining Quality Control: Ensure that any work outsourced meets your standards. Clear communication, detailed briefs, and regular check-ins can help maintain the quality of work while leveraging the talents of others.

Building a Personal Brand: Your Guiding Star

In the vast ocean of freelancing, your personal brand is the guiding star that attracts clients, collaborators, and opportunities. A strong, authentic personal brand can significantly amplify your efforts to scale your business.

Clarify Your Brand Message: Ensure your personal brand clearly communicates who you are, what you do, and the unique value you provide. This message should resonate through all your marketing materials, social media presence, and client interactions.

Visibility and Thought Leadership: Increase your visibility within your industry by sharing your knowledge, insights, and experiences. This could be through blogging, speaking at industry events, or engaging in online forums and social media discussions. Positioning yourself as a thought leader attracts higher-quality clients and opens up new opportunities for growth.

Networking and Relationships: Continue to invest in building and nurturing professional relationships. A strong network can be a significant growth lever, providing referrals, collaborations, and support as you scale your business.

Diversification: Exploring New Horizons

Scaling your freelance business often involves diversifying your income streams. This could mean expanding your service offerings, developing products, or exploring passive income opportunities.

Expand Your Services: Consider offering new services that complement your existing ones. For example, a graphic designer might expand into web design or branding services.

Productize Your Expertise: Turn your knowledge and expertise into products, such as courses, ebooks, or templates. These products can provide a source of passive income, reducing your reliance on trading time for money.

Explore New Markets: Look for opportunities to work with clients in different industries or geographic locations. This not only diversifies your income but also reduces the risk of market-specific downturns affecting your business.

Growth Mindset: The Captain's Compass

Adopting a growth mindset is essential when scaling your freelance business. Be prepared to face new challenges, learn from setbacks, and continuously adapt your strategies. Embrace the unknown with confidence and curiosity, viewing each obstacle as an opportunity to grow and learn.

Scaling Your Freelance Business: Embarking on a Grand Voyage

Scaling your freelance business is a grand voyage from the familiar comfort of solo projects to the exciting challenges of a growing enterprise. It requires a blend of strategic planning, delegation, strong personal branding, and a relentless pursuit of growth. By building a solid foundation, leveraging the talents of others, and continuously evolving your personal brand, you're not just expanding your business; you're embarking on an epic journey of professional and personal development. The seas of opportunity await, and the horizon is yours to explore.

CONCLUSION

The future of freelancing is a golden era, driven by technological advancements, shifting work paradigms, and global remote collaboration. The gig economy is evolving into a more sophisticated ecosystem, with professionals seeking deeper, more meaningful collaborations. Digital platforms and tools are becoming more integrated, making it easier to manage projects, connect with clients, and showcase talents globally. The increasing demand for specialized skills in emerging fields like artificial intelligence, sustainability, and digital marketing opens new frontiers for freelancers.

To stay relevant in this dynamic future, freelancers must cultivate a mindset of perpetual growth, constantly seeking to expand their knowledge and skills. They should also embrace the power of their personal brand, allowing it to shine brightly across the digital expanse, drawing clients and opportunities.

The world is becoming a playground for freelancers, allowing their dreams to take flight and ambitions to soar to new heights. As freelancers, dreamers, and doers, we must seize this moment with optimism and open minds to the endless possibilities that lie ahead.

Appendices

Resources for Freelancers

Below is a curated list of tools, websites, and communities designed to aid freelancers in various aspects of their work, from project management and financial tracking to skill development and networking.

Project Management and Collaboration Tools

Asana (asana.com): A versatile project management tool that helps freelancers organize tasks, projects, and deadlines with ease.

Trello (trello.com): A visual collaboration tool that uses boards, lists, and cards to organize and prioritize your projects in a fun, flexible way.

Slack (slack.com): A messaging app for teams that facilitates easy communication and file sharing, ideal for freelancers collaborating with clients or other freelancers.

Time Tracking and Invoicing

Harvest (getharvest.com): Offers time tracking and invoicing, making it easier for freelancers to manage billable hours and ensure timely payments.

FreshBooks (freshbooks.com): A cloud accounting software designed for freelancers and small business owners, offering invoicing, expense tracking, and time tracking.

Toggl (toggl.com): A simple time tracking tool that offers insightful reports into how you spend your working hours, helping optimize productivity.

Financial Management

QuickBooks (quickbooks.intuit.com): An accounting software solution that offers income and expense tracking, invoicing, and tax preparation tools.

Wave (waveapps.com): A free financial software designed for small businesses, providing invoicing, accounting, and receipt scanning functionalities.

Skill Development and Learning

Coursera (coursera.org): Offers online courses from top universities and companies, covering a wide range of topics relevant to freelancers.

Udemy (udemy.com): A global marketplace for learning and teaching online, where freelancers can expand their skill set in various fields.

LinkedIn Learning (linkedin.com/learning): Provides a wide array of video courses taught by industry experts in software, creative, and business skills.

Networking and Professional Communities

Behance (behance.net): An online platform to showcase and discover creative work, perfect for freelancers in creative fields seeking inspiration and community.

GitHub (github.com): An essential tool and community for developers to share code, work collaboratively, and build their portfolios.

Freelancers Union (freelancersunion.org): Offers solidarity, resources, and advocacy for freelancers, along with a platform for finding health insurance and other benefits.

Job Boards and Marketplaces

Upwork (upwork.com): One of the largest platforms for freelancers to find work across a wide range of skills and industries.

Fiverr (fiverr.com): An online marketplace for freelance services that caters to digital and creative professionals.

Toptal (toptal.com): Connects businesses with software engineers, designers, and business consultants who are among the top in their fields.

Inspirational and Educational Content

TED Talks (ted.com): Offers a plethora of inspirational talks from experts in various fields, providing insights, inspiration, and new perspectives.

Medium (medium.com): An open platform where freelancers can read, write, and engage with a wide range of articles written by experts and peers.

Portfolio Websites

Dribbble (dribbble.com): A community of designers sharing screenshots of their work, process, and projects, ideal for graphic designers and illustrators.

PortfolioBox (portfoliobox.net): A tool that allows freelancers to easily build a professional online portfolio.

This appendix serves as a compass, guiding freelancers through the myriad of tools and resources available to support their journey. By leveraging these resources, freelancers can enhance their productivity, expand their skill set, and connect with a vibrant community of like-minded professionals, setting the stage for a flourishing freelance career.

FAQs for Freelancers

1. How do I find my first freelance clients?

Start by leveraging your personal and professional networks to spread the word about your services. Create profiles on freelance marketplaces like Upwork, Fiverr, and LinkedIn to increase your visibility. Participating in relevant online forums and social media groups can also lead to potential client connections.

2. What should I include in my freelance contract?

Your contract should clearly outline the scope of work, deliverables, deadlines, payment terms, revision policies, and any confidentiality requirements. It's also wise to include clauses for cancellation terms and dispute resolution.

3. How do I set my freelance rates?

Consider factors like your experience, the complexity of the project, industry standards, and the value you bring to the client. Research what others in your field are charging and start with a rate that feels fair to both you and your client, adjusting as you gain more experience.

4. How can I manage irregular income in freelancing?

Create a budget that accounts for your average monthly expenses and aim to build an emergency fund that covers 3-6 months of living costs. During months with higher income, set aside savings to cushion slower periods.

5. How do I deal with scope creep in projects?

Clearly define the project scope and deliverables in your contract. If a client requests additional work outside the agreed scope, politely remind them of the contract terms and discuss the possibility of expanding the scope with corresponding adjustments to deadlines and fees.

6. What's the best way to manage multiple freelance projects simultaneously?

Use project management tools like Asana or Trello to keep track of tasks and deadlines. Prioritize work based on urgency and importance, and don't be afraid to communicate with clients if adjustments are needed.

7. How should I handle client feedback or revisions?

Establish a clear revision policy upfront, including how many rounds of revisions are included and any additional costs for extra revisions. Approach feedback positively, seeing it as an opportunity to refine your work and meet your client's needs more closely.

8. What are some tips for maintaining a work-life balance as a freelancer?

Set clear boundaries for your work hours and make time for breaks and personal activities. Learn to say no to projects that don't align with your goals or availability, and don't be afraid to outsource tasks to manage your workload better.

9. How do I increase my rates with existing clients?

Communicate your rate increase clearly and professionally, providing reasonable notice before the new rates take effect. Explain the reasons for the increase, focusing on the value and quality of your work, and be open to discussing any concerns your clients may have.

10. What should I do if a client is late with payment?

Refer to the payment terms in your contract and send a polite reminder shortly after the due date has passed. If payment is still not received, follow up with additional reminders, escalating the tone if necessary, and consider ceasing work until payment is made.

These FAQs are designed to provide a solid foundation for freelancers, offering guidance through common challenges and decisions. Remember, freelancing is a dynamic and evolving career path, and staying informed, adaptable, and proactive is key to navigating its waters successfully.

Appendix

Checklists and Templates for Freelancers

1. Freelance Business Setup Checklist

Define your service offerings and niche.

Choose a business name and register it, if necessary.

Set up a dedicated business bank account.

Create a professional website and portfolio.

Establish your social media presence in line with your professional brand.

Develop a basic contract template outlining your terms and conditions.

Set up an invoicing and accounting system.

Determine your rate structure (hourly, project-based, retainer).

Invest in necessary equipment and software tools.

Join relevant professional networks and online communities.

2. Pitch and Proposal Template

Introduction: Briefly introduce yourself and your freelance business, highlighting your experience and areas of expertise.

Understanding the Client's Needs: Summarize your understanding of the client's project and objectives, demonstrating your attention to their needs.

Proposed Solution: Outline your approach to the project, including key deliverables, methodologies, and how your solution addresses the client's needs.

Timeline: Provide a tentative project timeline, detailing major milestones and estimated completion dates.

Investment and Rates: Clearly outline your pricing structure, including any packages or options available to the client.

Previous Work Samples: Include links or attachments showcasing your previous work relevant to the client's project.

Next Steps: Detail the next steps if the client wishes to proceed, including how to get in touch, contract signing, and initial payment.

Closing: Conclude with a thank you note, expressing your enthusiasm about the possibility of working together.

3. Personal Branding Guide

Identify your unique value proposition: What makes you stand out in your field?

Define your target audience: Who are your ideal clients?

Develop a consistent visual identity: Logo, color scheme, and typography.

Craft your professional bio: A concise narrative that highlights your background, skills, and what you bring to your clients.

Optimize your online presence: Ensure your website, portfolio, and social media profiles are cohesive and reflect your personal brand.

Content strategy: Plan the types of content you'll create to demonstrate your expertise, such as blog posts, case studies, or social media posts.

Networking plan: Identify key events, online communities, and platforms where you can engage with your target audience and peers.

4. Daily and Weekly Planner Templates

Daily Planner:

Top 3 priorities for the day

Schedule of tasks and meetings, with time blocks

Notes section for ideas and reminders

End-of-day review: Accomplishments and areas for improvement

Weekly Planner:

Weekly goals aligned with long-term objectives

Key tasks for the week, categorized by project/client

Personal development time (learning, networking)

Weekly review: Successes, challenges, and next week's focus

5. Financial Management Checklist

Track all income and business expenses diligently.

Set aside a percentage of each payment for taxes.

Regularly invoice clients, following clear payment terms.

Conduct a monthly financial review: income, expenses, and budget adjustments.

Allocate funds for an emergency savings account.

Plan for retirement savings and other long-term financial goals.

Review and update your pricing strategy annually or as needed.

These checklists and templates are designed to be starting points, adaptable to the specific needs and nuances of your freelance business. By incorporating these tools into your workflow, you can create a more structured, efficient, and professional freelance practice, allowing you to focus more on what you do best—delivering exceptional value to your clients.